ONLY

KITCHENS & ACCESSORIES

Editor-in-Chief
ALEJANDRO ASENSIO

Subeditor and texts
EVA MARÍN

Art Editor
MIREIA FABREGAS

Editorial Staff
MARC GRAU
ROBERTA VELLINI
XAVIER ROSELLÓ
CARLOS RIVERO

Photographic Documentation
SEAN ROVIRA
ASTRID MARTEEN
DANIEL JARAMILLO

Production Director
JUANJO RODRÍGUEZ NOVEL

Design and Layout
MANEL PERET
JORDI CALLEJA

Infographics
TONI LLADÓ FERNÁNDEZ
ENRIC NAVARRO
MANEL PERET

Traduction
MARK HOLLOWAY
MARGARIDA RIBEIRO
DAVID SUTCLIFFE

Copyright © 2004 Atrium Group
Published by:
Atrium Group de ediciones y publicaciones S.L.
Ganduxer, 112
08022 Barcelona

Tel: +34 932 540 099
Fax: +34 932 118 139
e-mail: atrium@atriumgroup.org
www.atriumbooks.com

ISBN: 84-96099-54-7
D.L.: B-47.146-2004

Printed in Spain
Ferré Olsina S.A.

INDEX

This is, maybe, the most conventional distribution that there is. On occasions, when the available space is long and narrow or simply small, it is often the only possible option. The single file kitchen incorporates cupboards set in line against the wall. The storage models are situated in two parallel files in the upper and lower areas. Another possibility is that of the L-kitchen which equips adjacent walls and allows for more cupboards and drawers to be incorporated while leaving the central zone free. On the following pages, we will see different proposals for how to make the most of the corner areas such as by using them for the washing or cooking zone.

When there is a large amount of space available for the kitchen, this type of distribution is very practical. The islands function as work areas that are clearly differentiated from the others, but that integrate to perfection. In these independent modules, the water or cooking zone can be situated so that there is plenty of room for each task to be undertaken in comfort. Part of this worktop can also be made use of for a breakfast bar if there is not enough room to fit in a table.

The Aztecs introduced the concept of the kitchen/dining area which was situated in the center of the house where the fire burnt day and night. Eat-in kitchens, popularly considered to be American in style, continue this philosophy of situating the cooking appliance in the center of the house and uniting it with the public areas in a continual flow. It is one of the models that adapts most to contemporary architecture in which walls disappear and are substituted by other more flexible divisions.

General introduction

In recent years, the kitchen has become the most important space in the home. Some time ago, there was a tendency to reduce its dimensions when it came to designing new homes. However, nowadays, it is being made larger because it is not only a work area of daily use, but also a meeting place in which people get together before, during and after meals. When designing a new kitchen, it is essential to take into account not only the number of people who will be using it, but their lifestyle as well. It is true that a single person has different necessities with respect to a couple with children, but a diversity of factors should also be borne in mind, for example, whether or not there are frequently guests for supper. Nowadays, there are many offers on the market destined to making the most of this area of the home. It is not simply a question of making the most of the available space, but also one of aesthetics given that this is a space for meeting and, consequently, an effort is made to create an atmosphere dominated by order, logic and beauty. However, it is also a place used for work on a daily basis so the way the multitude of complements and accessories are integrated into cupboards, drawers and islands that facilitate the daily task of cooking should be organized down to the smallest detail. Ergonomics are being applied more and more efficiently and are minimizing the impact of uncomfortable postures and accidents with new dimensions, dispositions and heights which are more adaptable to the user's anatomy. Over 100 companies in this sector show us their latest models in which the new technologies and good design make it possible to create kitchens to live in.

single file

This is, maybe, the most conventional distribution that there is. On occasions, when the available space is long and narrow or simply small, it is often the only possible option. The single file kitchen incorporates cupboards set in line against the wall. The storage models are situated in two parallel files in the upper and lower areas. Another possibility is that of the L-kitchen which equips adjacent walls and allows for more cupboards and drawers to be incorporated while leaving the central zone free. On the following pages, we will see different proposals for how to make the most of the corner areas such as by using them for the washing or cooking zone. Below these areas, a cupboard for pots and pans that rotates and that can be pulled out maximizes the usefulness of the space. In this sort of kitchen, the ideal place for the breakfast counter tends to be one of these angles. Here, stalls, folding chairs or a sliding bench can be installed according to the space available and requirements. Lastly, there is the U-kitchen that uses three walls and provides a fluid space to cook in. The models that we will see on the pages that follow represent a diversity of styles ranging from classical to rustic or to the latest tendencies. However, in all cases, they are designs that offer the most innovative solutions to storage spaces and to the working areas of the kitchen.

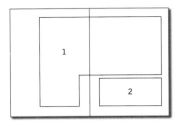

1. Model from BINOVA that belongs to the collection of Technological Kitchens: Index.
2. Detail of one of the shelves from
   Index with incorporated light.

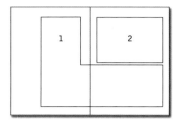

1. More details of the cooking zone, cupboards and organizer storage drawers from the model Index designed by Paolo Nava and Fabio Casiraghi and produced by BINOVA.

2. Model Index from BINOVA.

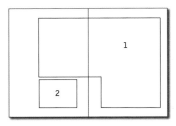

1. Aother two possible combinations of the model Index from BINO-VA.
2. Detail of the hotplates arranged in single file.

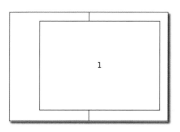

1. Different details and two combinations of this model from SIRA CUCINE: Sydney with lacquered finishes in white.

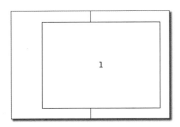

1. SIRA CUCINE includes the model Giorgia in its catalog in cherry wood.

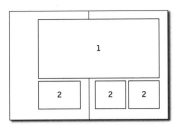

1. Another version of the model Giorgia in cherry wood from SIRA CUCINE.

2. Two details of the first model.

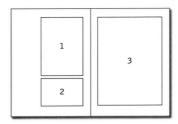

1. TECTA include the Küchenbaum from Stefan Wewerka in their catalog, a very versatile accessory.

2. Hangers from the firm ARRMET, Gino.

3. Different finishes of the model Tabula from EUROMOBIL.

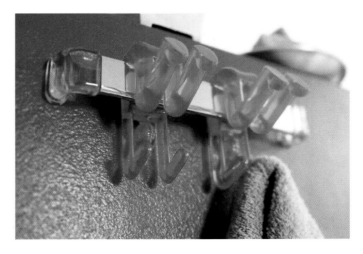

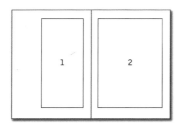

1. VINÇON propose these two combinations with different surfaces and accessories.

2. Different finishes of the model Quadri produced by EUROMOBIL.

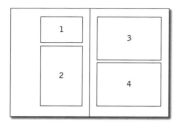

1. A chair from MATTEOGRASSI designed by Luigi Massoni: Elisa.
2. BONALDO produce the stool Hoppy from Giorgio Manzali.
3. Model Dogano from EUROMO-BIL.
4. The chair Elisa from MAT-TEOGRASSI in white.

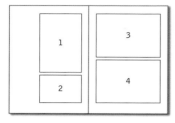

1. A detail of the water zone of the model Ginger from ARCLINEA.
2. Container from the brand PHILIPP PLEIN.
3. EUROMOBIL produce the model Alutem.
4. A combination of Ginger from the brand ARCLINEA.

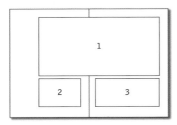

1. Italia is a proposal from AR-CLINEA.

2. Detail of one of the organizer drawers for storing knives and other utensils.

3. Container and cooking zone from the firm PHILIPP PLEIN.

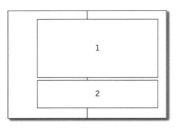

1. ARCLINEA present the model Florida.
2. Detail of the water and cooking zones (left) and the bins for recycling (right).

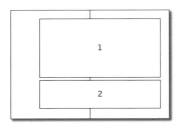

1. Alis Catania is a proposal from the firm ARCLINEA.

2. Various details of the model featured above.

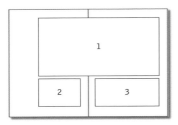

1. Model Alis Siviglia from AR-
   CLINEA.
2. Detail of the stool Hoppy from
   the firm BONALDO.
3. Container and island for water
   zone from PHILIPP PLEIN.

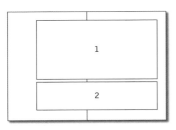

1. ARCLINEA present this combination of the model Hetta Bologna.

2. Details of the water and cooking zones and of the shelving for storage from the model in Image #1.

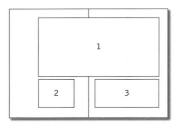

1. Designed by Paolo Nava and Fabio Casiraghi, Continua is a technological kitchen from BINOVA.

2. Detail of one of the cupboards of Continua.

3. Another possible combination of Continua from BINOVA.

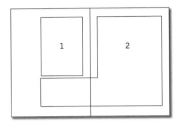

1. Detail of a storage shelf from the model Continua from BINOVA.

2. The drawers in the model Continua are situated in the lower areas.

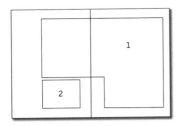

1. A proposal from SIRA CUCINE in a rustic style: Emma with lacquered finishes in light yellow.

2. Detail of the water zones from the model Emma.

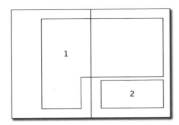

1. Emma from SIRA CUCINE in lacquered white.

2. Detail of the working area with shelves (left) and the cooking zone (right).

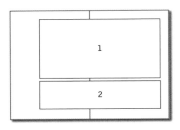

1. Alexa with finishes in anodized aluminum and lacquered panel from SIRA CUCINE.
2. Detail of the cooking zone (left), drawers (center) and sink (right).

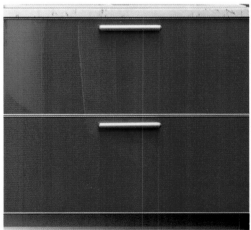

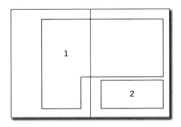

1. SIRA CUCINE also present Alexia in laminas of stratified daffodil.

2. A detail of the hotplates (left) and one of the drawers for utensils (right).

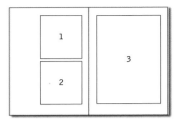

1. Stool from the firm BONALDO, Mirtillo, designed by Peter Ross.
2. Colored hangers from ARRMET, Gino.
3. Eurococina 2004 was designed by Lorenzo Tondelli for ABC KITCHENS.

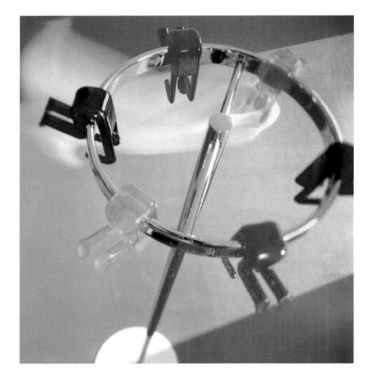

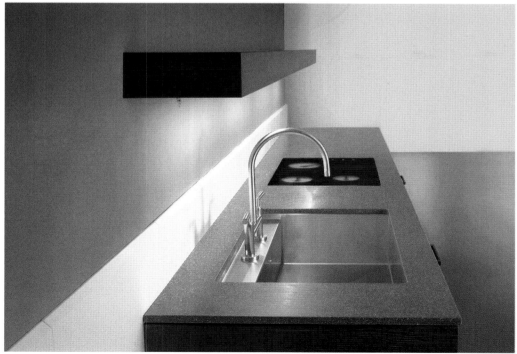

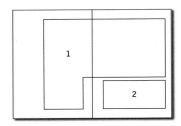

1. Models Habit (on this page) and Planet (on the following page) from VARENNA.

2. NOBILIA present Alba 547.

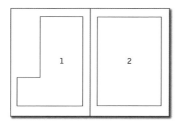

1. VARENNA include this design from Studio Kairos in their catalog: Tecna.
2. Kitchens form the firm NOBILIA. Alba 549 (top) and Arte 522 (bottom).

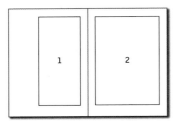

1. NOBILIA commercialize the model Finca 554.

2. Time in different finishes. It is a proposal from VARENNA.

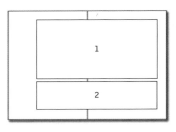

1. The Fiona 347 is another product from NOBILIA.

2. Also from NOBILIA, the Clássico 395. In the photograph on the left, a detail of the cupboards with glass fronts.

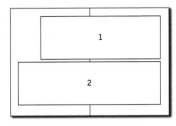

1. The model City 540 from NO-BILIA. In the photograph on the left, a detail of the storage cupboards with slatted-shutter doors.

2. Other proposals from NOBILIA: Contura 376 (left) and Castello 397 (right).

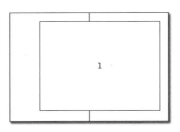

1. From NOBILIA's Catalog, on this page the model Grado 544. On the following at the top, City 513 and below the model Cosmos 347.

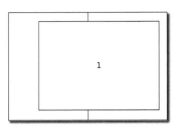

1. Alongside these lines: Lugano 339, another model from the firm NOBILIA. On the following page, top, Lido 399 and, below, Lugano 366.

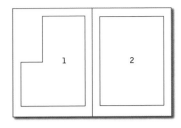

1. Pia 538 is a proposal from NO-BILIA. Next to these lines, a detail of one of the cupboards for pots and pans with sliding door.

2. Two versions of the model Natura from NOBILIA: above the 370 and below the 302.

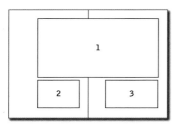

1. NOBILIA present this combination of Pia 531.

2. A draw for storing kitchen knives and cutlery in an organized fashion from the firm NOBILIA.

3. Detail of the pull out spice rack (left) and the wooden organizer drawers for kitchen knives and cutlery (right), both from NOBILIA.

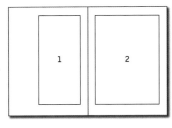

1. A design with more classical airs produced by NOBILIA, the model Romántica 529. Next to these lines, a detail of the larder.

2. Two versions of Reno from the same make. Top, the 379 and, bottom, the 532.

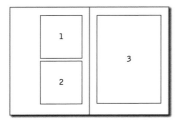

1. A storage cupboard with pull out shelves from NOBILIA.

2. Swing 568 with finishes in white from the same make.

3. Above, a combination of Swing 567 and below Tehno 344, also from NOBILIA.

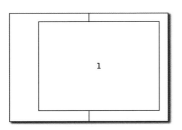

1. NOBILIA propose model Uno 523. Below, the interior aspect of the different storage spaces (left), a detail of the oven and storage drawers (center), and a pull out cupboard.

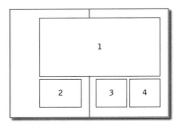

1. A model from NOBILIA.

2. A module from the same firm in aluminum and glass.

3. Detail of corner water zone and cupboard with waste separator on a rotating base, also from NOBILIA.

4. Corner pull out cupboard.

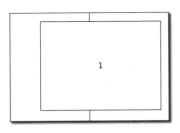

1. Different proposals from NOBIL-IA for storage with organizers for utensils, cleaning products, household bits and pieces and food which guarantees to make the most of every nook and cranny.

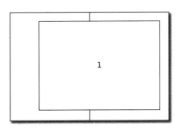

1

1. C A S A W E L L - S E R V I C E
   GRUPPE propose this model
   from the brand Wellmann. Below,
   a detail of the table (left) and of
   the cupboards for food (center)
   and for household things (right).

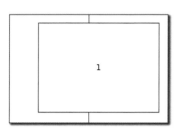

1. C A S A W E L L - S E R V I C E
GRUPPE present the model
Wellmann which incorporates the
new technologies and takes care
of the very last detail with versatile accessories.

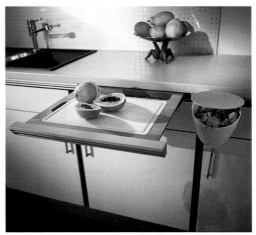

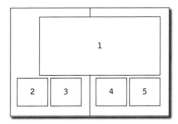

1. Another proposal from CA-SAWELL SERVICE GRUPPE and Wellmann. All of the photographs on this page are of the same model.

2. Detail of the illumination system incorporated into the cupboards.

3. A bin for recycling that uses a pull out drawer system.

4. Cupboards with glass doors which are comfortable to open and close.

5. These semitransparent drawers, set at different heights, make the contents partially visible.

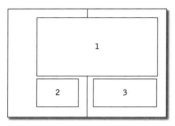

1. Another combination of a model from the firm Wellmann that belongs to CASAWELL SERVICE GRUPPE.

2. Detail of the upper cupboards with three shelves.

3. The drawers in this model maximize storage space thanks to the organizers.

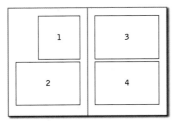

1. CASAWELL SERVICE GRUP-
   PE present different kitchen models from Wellmann in the four
   photographs on this page.

2. Placing the cooking zone in the
   corner allows for an optimum use
   of space to be made.

3. The cooker incorporates a bar on
   which to hang the spice rack,
   cloths and utensils in a practical
   way.

4. A less conventional furnishing option for the kitchen, also from
   Wellmann.

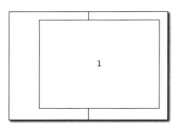

1. Different models from the Wellmann brand of CASAWELL
SERVICE GRUPPE.

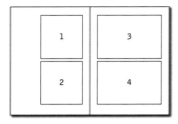

1. On this page, various Wellmann models from CASAWELL SERVICE GRUPPE. In this photograph, furniture for young atmospheres.

2. Some elements remain on view when the cupboards are alternated with shelving.

3. In this proposal from CASAWELL, the cooker hood fulfils the function of a small shelf.

4. A model from the brand Wellmann with a more classical air.

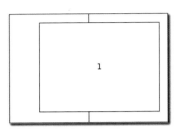

1. The brand WELLMANN offer a great variety of kitchens which propose solutions for different necessities in a diversity of aesthetics and in a range of finishes to choose from.

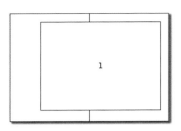

1. Also from the brand WELL-MANN four different models for the kitchen. On this page, top, over the cooking zone various options when it comes to hanging up the utensils that are most frequently used.

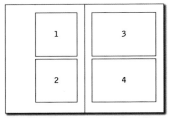

1. VALCUCINE present the model Artematica which is reminiscent of Japanese culture and aesthetics. Pure lines, high quality materials and functionality stand out in the products of this make.

2. The model Artematica with finishes in red.

3. Another proposal from VALCUCINE which combines aluminum with color. The shelves in wood introduce a touch of warmth.

4. VALCUCINE produce this kitchen with a minimalist line in which both design and functionality are found.

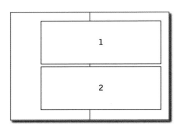

1. Model Alenza from BLOCK
   COCINAS. On the left, details of
   the drawers, which combine aluminum and wood, and of the work
   surface.

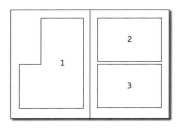

1. DONNA COCINAS present the model Cadiz. In the two photographs next these lines a detail of the bottle rack and one of the organizer drawers for pots and pans.

2. A kitchen from GAMADECOR and PORCELANOSA with finishes in wenge.

3. Another proposal from GAMADECOR and PORCELANOSA in light tones, very versatile.

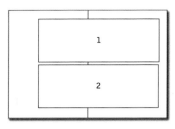

1. MOBALCO produce the kitchen Forma 400.

2. AURÓ present the model Omega in simple lines and with cared for details. The pull out cupboards and drawers (left) facilitate maximum organization.

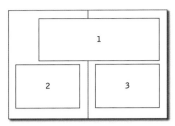

1. Kuba is a product from CUCINE COPAT elaborated in high quality materials and of an elegant and contemporary design.

2. Cucina Bianca from DRIADE.

3. Also from the brand DRIADE, the model Kuoko.

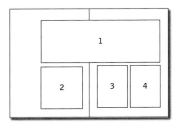

1. A model from BLOCK COCINAS finished in lilac.
2. Detail of the water and cooking zones.
3. One of the drawers in which to store kitchen utensils which also makes use of the space in the base of the unit.
4. The recycling bins are integrated into this pull out cupboard.

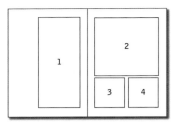

1. A small cupboard with wicker drawers on rollers and a very flexible module for working or dining on which is also a cupboard with pull out pieces with a large storage capacity from BLOCK COCINAS.

2. The water and cooking zone from the same model from BLOCK COCINAS.

3. This independent cupboard with built-in light is one of the options offered by this kitchen.

4. Two details: one of the glass cupboards with raising doors and interior lights and, below, one of the cooker hood and metal shelves from the same model.

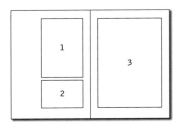

1. Orotava is another product from the catalog of BLOCK COCINAS.

2. Detail of one of the pull out cupboards with shelves (left) and built-in microwave oven (right) from the model Orotava.

3. Model Oda, rustic in style and also from the brand BLOCK COCINAS. Below on the left, lace curtains hide a pull out shelf.

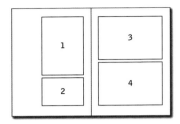

1. Pantry from the Valsacro model produced by BLOCK COCINAS.

2. Detail of a worktable Valsacro.

3. Valsacro is another proposal from the firm BLOCK COCINAS for rustic atmospheres.

4. Two details from the same model from BLOCK COCINAS.

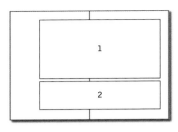

1. DONNA COCINAS present this kitchen: Escorial.

2. Detail of one of the drawers from Escorial with organizer (left), the cooker hood (center) and pull out shelves (right).

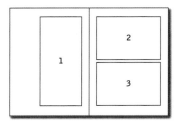

1. Two options for storage from the make MOBALCO. Model Forma 400. Top, a cupboard with glass doors and metal shelves and, below, another piece of furniture with six doors and with metal shelves on both sides.

2. A possible combination of the kitchen Forma 400 from MOBALCO.

3. Detail of one of the glass cabinets for the china (left) and of the transparent handles (right).

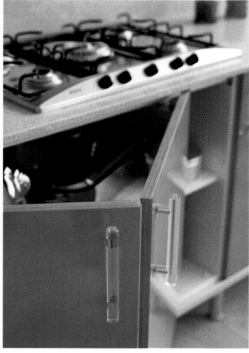

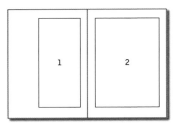

1. A proposal of a classical style from OSTER.

2. Model Cambridge, also from the brand OSTER. Below, a detail of the work island. The furniture reproduces a classical rustic style.

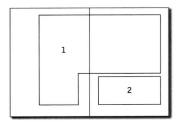

1. On this page, the model Altea and on the following the Boston, both from the company BOSSIA.

2. A product from the DADA catalog (photograph conceded by AR-CAYA EQUIP).

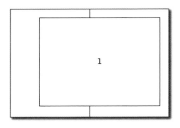

1. Various proposals for the kitchen from DADA. All with a purity of line and sober elegance.

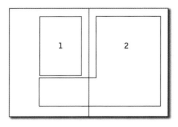

1. Cooking zone from the model Kila Basic LH1 from ELMAR CUCINE.

2. Different combinations and colors of the model Kila Basic LH1 from the brand ELMAR.

with island

When there is a large amount of space available for the kitchen, this type of distribution is very practical. The islands function as work areas that are clearly differentiated from the others, but that integrate to perfection. In these independent modules, the water or cooking zone can be situated so that there is plenty of room for each task to be undertaken in comfort. Part of this worktop can also be made use of for a breakfast bar if there is not enough room to fit in a table. In this section, different brands propose all sorts of solutions for this area. Some brands incorporate kitchen sink and plate rack in the same piece. Other designs divide the sink into a large bowl and another smaller one for washing vegetables. From among the accessories, the insertable mesh trays are a very helpful resource when it comes to making the most of the island's work surface. Other models include small bowls that fit into the structure for organic waste. The faucets may range from conventional single-lever or twin-handled mixers to those with very practical long spouts although there are the extractable models that are most flexible and allow work to be carried out in the greatest comfort. Completely flat vitroceramic hobs and others with gas rings, there are those who prefer the cooked-over-a-fire flavor while others give priority to aesthetics and what is practical. This chapter brings together the most professional kitchens for the domestic environment.

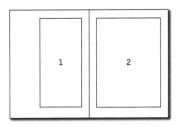

1. Artusi is a product from AR-CLINEA.
2. The company EUROMOBIL propose the model Dogano.

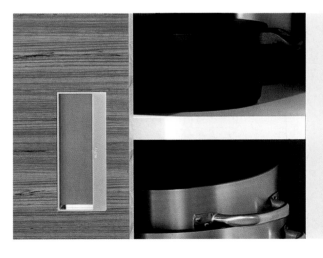

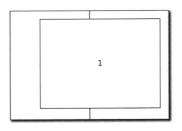

1. ARCLINEA include the models
   Artusi (on this page and on the
   following, bottom) and Convivium
   (top, right) in their catalog.

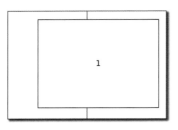

1. On this page, different details of the model Convivium from AR-CLINEA are shown.

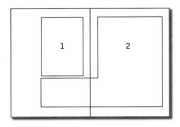

1. Another proposal from the firm ARCLINEA, the kitchen Mediter-ránea, which includes a ladder on a guide for easy access to the higher cupboards.

2. Different details of the same mo-del from ARCLINEA.

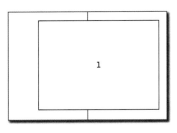

1. BINOVA include this kitchen with island in their catalog in different finishes. Country is a design by Paolo Nava.

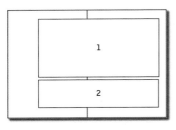

1. Paolo Nava and Fabio Casiraghi designed the model Index for BI-NOVA.

2. Various details of Prima. Another proposal from BINOVA created by Paolo Nava and Fabio Casiraghi.

.

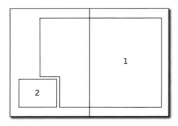

1. Various combinations of the model Prima from BINOVA with the cooking zone and water zone in different positions.

2. Details of the model Regula also designed by Paolo Nava and Fabio Casiraghi for BINOVA.

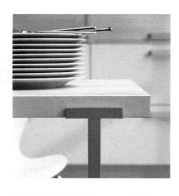

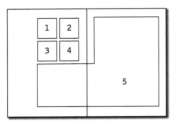

1. Trays My 080 from the firm MAGIS and designed by Michael Young.

2. Colorful Captain Lovetray trays which are included in the catalog from MAGIS. They were created by Jerszy Seymour.

3. Stackable bottle rack Bottle from Jasper Morrison for MAGIS.

4. Andries & Hiroko van Onck designed these trolleys with wheels which are also from MAGIS: Dove.

5. Kitchen with island Regula from BINOVA.

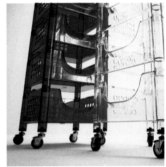

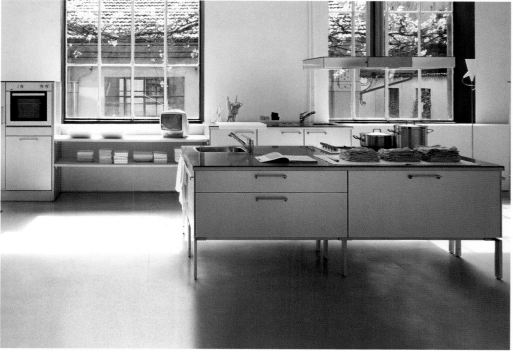

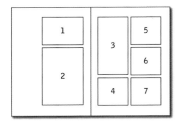

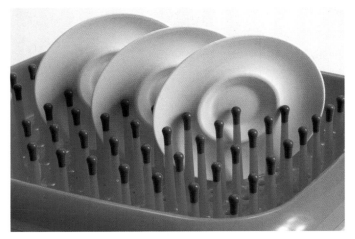

1. MAGIS include this design from Mark Newson in their catalog.

2. Jasper Morrison designed this cutlery holder from MAGIS.

3. Worktop from the company CO-SENTINO.

4. Small wooden containers from BLOCK COCINAS.

5. BLOCK COCINAS produce this product: Merlot.

6. Wicker drawer Valsacro from BLOCK COCINAS.

7. Rioja is another proposal from BLOCK COCINAS.

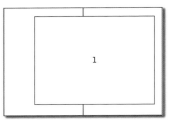

1. The electrical appliances are almost hidden in the kitchen Sydney in wengue in this photograph. It is a product from SIRA CUCINE. Minimalist design and elegance stand out in this model.

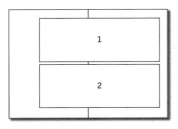

1. The model Aurora finished in white is a proposal from SIRA CUCINE.

2. Aurora from SIRA CUCINE in laminated cherry wood. On the left, the sink with a variety of recipients for the different tasks of the water zone. The knives are at hand which reduces the risk of accidents.

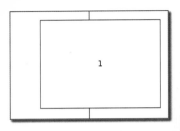

1. ABC KITCHENS present this design from Lorenzo Tondelli with minimalist airs.

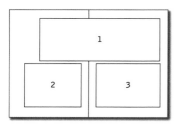

1. Model Alba 548 from NOBILIA. Next to these lines, a detail of the sideboard.

2. Also from NOBILIA, the model Pia 530.

3. Another version of Pia, the model 537.

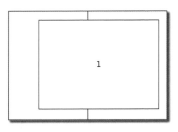

1. Four proposals for kitchens with islands in different styles from the brand WELLMANN of the CASAWELL group.

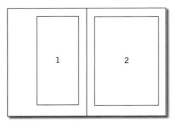

1. BLOCK COCINAS propose this shelf and set of drawers alogside the water and cooking zones. The design of this model allows for a extraordinary distribution.

2. Two versions of the model Artematica from VALCUCINE.

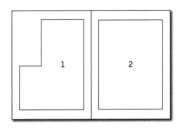

1. The company TONCELLI present Credenza.

2. Two proposals from GAMADE-COR and PORCELANOSA. Top, the model G 640 and bottom, the G 210.

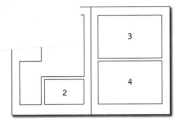

1. Kitchen Natia from the brand TONCELLI.
2. A detail from the model Living from TONCELLI.
3. Island and cupboard with shelves Living.
4. Avantgarde is a product from MOBALCO.

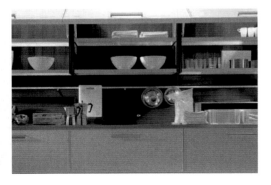

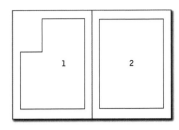

1. A proposal from MOBALCO: Avantgarde. Below these lines some details of the finishes and of the interiors of the drawers with organizers for plates and cutlery.

2. DONNA COCINAS present the model Escorial with work island.

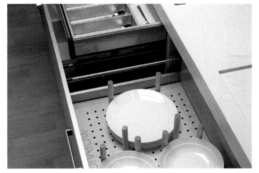

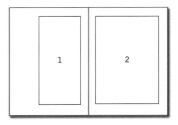

1. Achillea is a product from DRI-AFROM .

2. Extractors from the brand ELI-CA. From top to bottom, in the column on the left, the models: Antart, Atlant and Menhir. On the right: Concav and Antart.

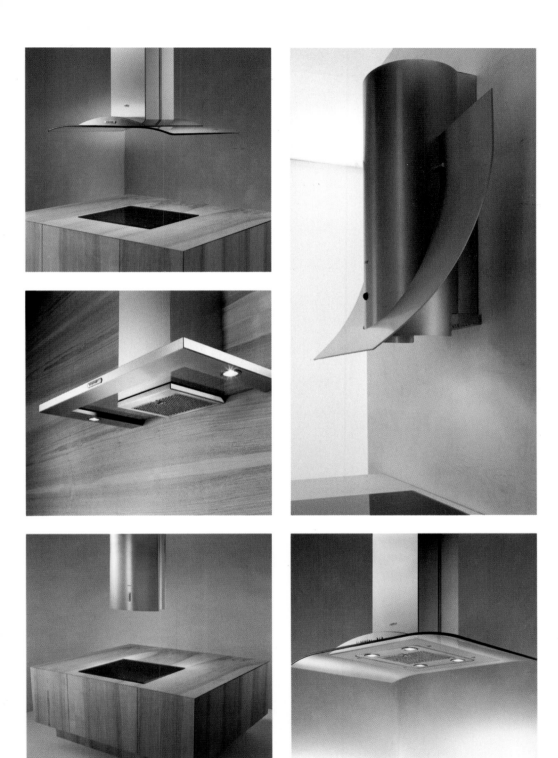

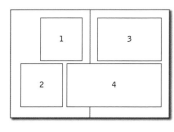

1. Refrigerators from the brand SMEG.

2. Kuoko ad Isola produced by DRIADE.

3. Another version of Kuoko ad Isola from DRIADE.

4. CUCINE COPAT present the model Mar.

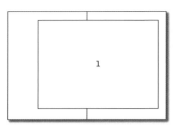

1. Different products from the DADA catalog with minimalist airs.

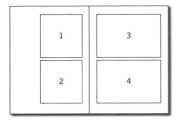

1. BIS BIS KITCHENS propose this Kitchen in a rustic style.
2. A kitchen with island from the brand DADA.
3. ALNO produce the model Alnojet in a cream color.
4. A model from the DADA catalog.

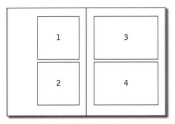

1. Cooking zone and bar from the brand BIS BIS KITCHENS.

2. ELMAR CUCINE present this island as a novelty in the Eurococina of 2004.

3. Kitchen from the brand DADA.

4. Another composition from BIS BIS KITCHENS.

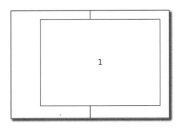

1. Frame is a product from ELMAR
   CUCINE who take great care of
   details so as to be able to cook
   like professions.

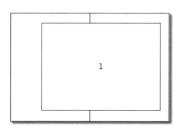

1. Sinks and faucets from the brand FRANKE.

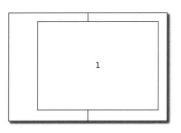

1. The model LA 656 from the company POGGENPOHL.

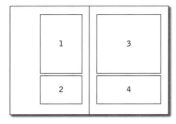

1. POGGENPOHL propose this model with island.

2. Detail of one of the drawers with organizer for aluminum paper and recipients for food from the model in photograph 1.

3. Another proposal from the brand POGGENPOHL.

4. Kitchen Largo from LEICHT.

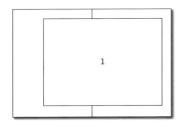

1. Drawer organizers from the model Viva produced by LEICHT.

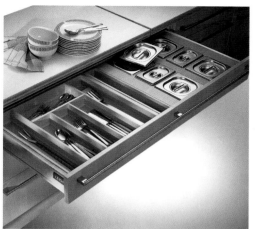

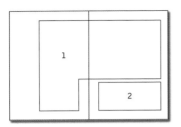

1. Studio Kairos designed the kitchen Tecna for VARENNA.

2. Sink and oven island from the model Tecna.

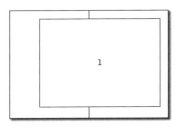

1. NOBILIA propose the models Pia 345 (top), Trend 343 (bottom), next to these lines and, on the following page Fina 100 (top) and Grado 527 (bottom).

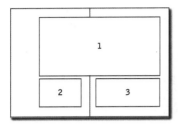

1. BLOCK COCINAS produce the model Merlot.

2. Detail of some of the wicker drawers from the kitchen Merlot.

3. Cupboards and cooking zone from the same model from BLOCK COCINAS.

1. ALNO produce the model High Gloss Black.

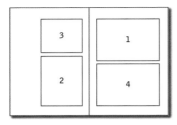

1. Futura is a proposal from MOBALCO.

2. The water zone and the cooking zone from the model Futura.

3. One of the drawer organizers of Futura from the brand MOBAL-CO.

4. Detail of island doors from the model Futura.

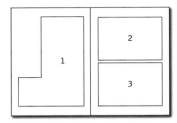

1. A model from DADA in red and white.

2. Alno Grand Red.

3. Iride is a product from CUCINE COPAT.

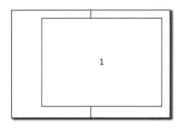

1. BIS BIS KITCHENS present these models.

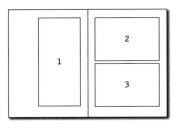

1. Model Kila Basic from ELMAR
   CUCINE.

2. Another proposal from ELMAR
   CUCINE with elegant pure lines.

3. Alno Grand Blue is a kitchen
   from the ALNO catalog.

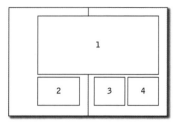

1. Alnoline pro Natural in cherry wood from the brand ALNO.

2. Detail of one of the drawers for cutlery.

3. By means of using the same finish for the door as has been used for the other furniture, the refrigerator has been completely assimilated into this proposal from the company ALNO.

4. Another detail from the same model from ALNO.

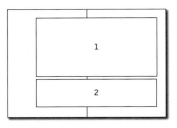

1. Alnotec pro High-Gloss in brilliant white, with finishes in matt aluminum. It is a model produced by ALNO.

2. Various details from the same model from ALNO: drawer organizers (left), faucet with pull out flexible tube (center) and different types of drawers (the two photographs on the right).

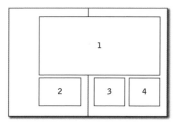

1. A proposal from ALNO: Alnotec pro High-Gloss in brilliant red with finishes in matt aluminum.

2. This model from ALNO proposes an easy way to keep knives at hand, but not necessarily on view.

3. Detail of the drawers with organizers for various uses.

4. Amplitude is one of the characteristics of Alnotec pro High-Gloss.

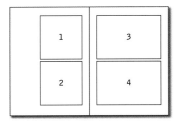

1. Island from the brand PHILIPP PLEIN.

2. The kitchen Alutem is a proposal from the company EUROMOBIL.

3. CESAR produce the model Coco, in the photograph in white.

4. Another version from the model Coco with finishes in aluminum.

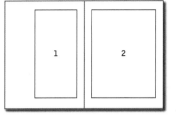

1. The model Alnojet Azure Blue from the brand ALNO.

2. The company ALNO produce this kitchen: Alnojet Simulated Ripled Aluminium.

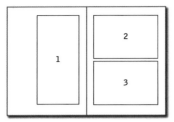

1. Evolution is a proposal from TONCELLI.

2. CESAR produce the model Zoe Ciliegio.

3. THE SINGULAR KITCHEN present Trend with finishes in aluminum and blue laminate.

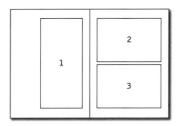

1. CESAR present the model Zoe, designed by G. V. Plazzogna, in cherry wood (top) and oak (bottom).

2. Titel Pia is a kitchen from NOBILIA.

3. THE SINGULAR KITCHEN propose the model Pia with Sahara 530 doors.

eat-in

The Aztecs introduced the concept of the kitchen/dining area which was situated in the center of the house where the fire burnt day and night. Eat-in kitchens, popularly considered to be American in style, continue this philosophy of situating the cooking appliance in the center of the house and uniting it with the public areas in a continual flow. It is one of the models that adapts most to contemporary architecture in which walls disappear and are substituted by other more flexible divisions. These modules separate atmospheres but allow for communication as they leave the upper part of the area visible while partially hiding the work zone. They also provide ideal distributions for smaller rectangular spaces as they can be used as much for dining as for working on. Over these elements, shelves or small cupboards can be installed to store crockery and so on to make good use of every corner. On the following pages, we will show a great diversity of proposals presently available on the market and different ways of making the most of them in different sorts of kitchen whether they are the more conventional versions, close to high narrow tables, L-shaped or the type that are partially closed and that offer storage space.

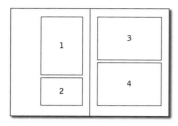

1. A cupboard from the brand AR-CLINEA, model Iller Barcelona.
2. Grado 545, an original proposal from NOBILIA.
3. Kitchen Iller Barcelona from the ARCLINEA catalog.
4. ARCLINEA present Bonjour Parigi.

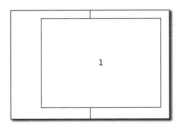

1. Different kitchens from the brand ARCLINEA. From top to bottom, on this page, Weiss Berlino and Weiss Cannes. On the following, Inner Milano and Nest Stoccolma.

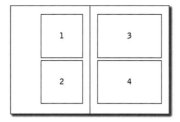

1. Black Ga is one of the latest proposals from POGGENPOHL.
2. Black Zebrano W06 is another product from POGGENPOHL.
3. Another product from POGGENPOHL.
4. G. V. Plazzogna designed the model Coco for CESAR.

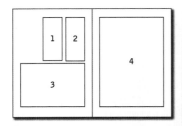

1. The glass door "hielo" opens with a mechanism that allows for the most to be made of the available space in the model Coco from CESAR.

2. Cooker hood and built in oven from the kitchen Coco from CESAR.

3. CESAR produce the model Coco in oak and glass door "hielo". In the photograph, the combination includes a work island.

4. G. V. Plazzognal designed the model Coco for CESAR. In this case, the island includes water and cooking zones.

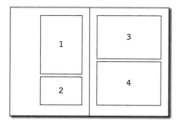

1. Island from the model Coco Millerighe in white.

2. Detail from the model Coco Millerighe in aluminum.

3. A combination of Coco Millerighe in white with two islands.

4. An island from Coco Millerighe in aluminum.

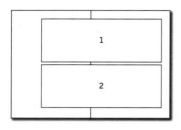

1. Another version in oak of Coco from CESAR.

2. Model Coco with glass "amaranth".

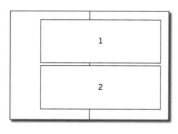

1. Model Aria in oak from CESAR.
2. Aria is also available in cream and orange.

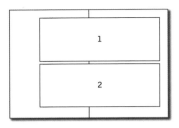

1. Aria from CESAR in white.
2. CESAR also produce the model Frida in wengue. The pull out cupboards (photograph on the left) help make full use of the available space.

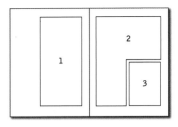

1. Frida from CESAR is also available in brilliant white.

2. From the brand CESAR, the model Zoe in oak.

3. CESAR also produce Zoe in cherry.

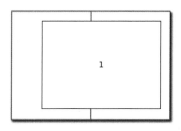

1. BLUM offer different options when it comes to organizing the drawers with all sorts of different types of utensils, foods and household equipment in mind.

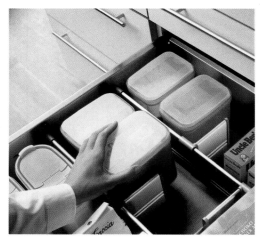

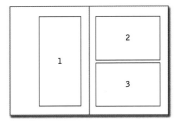

1. Two models from the brand POGGENPOHL.

2. LEICHT produce the kitchen Orlando.

3. Different products from the SMEG catalog.

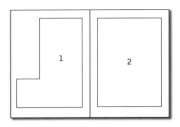

1. LEICHT produce the model Akzent.

2. Two combinations of the kitchen Castello from the brand LEICHT.

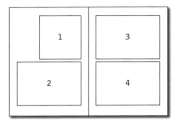

1. THE SINGULAR KITCHEN present the model Swing, in the photograph with doors in Lava 567.

2. Model Natura with doors in Light Beech produced by THE SINGULAR KITCHEN.

3. Evolution is a product from TONCELLI.

4. Model Swing from THE SINGULAR KITCHEN with doors Silver 568.

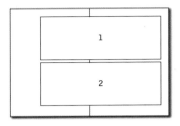

1. VARENNA propose this design from Paolo Piva: Alea.

2. Model Habit from VARENNA.

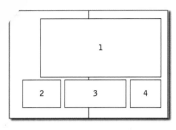

1. The model Natura 370 from NO-BILIA.
2. A product from the brand SMEG.
3. A detail of the hotplates from the model Inner Barcelona from AR-CLINEA.
4. An oven from SMEG.

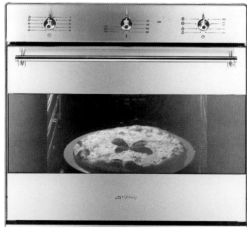

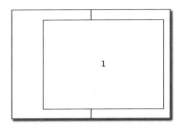

1. Different proposals of ARCAYA
   EQUIP from the brand DADA.

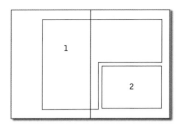

1. BIS BIS KITCHENS propose these kitchens in various styles.

2. Kila Basic is a product from EL-MAR CUCINE.

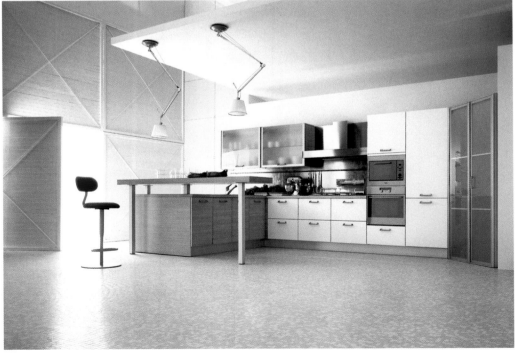

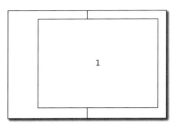

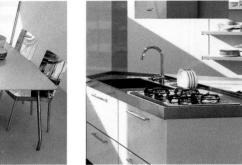

1. Different details of the model Frame from ELMAR CUCINE.

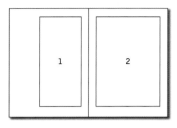

1. Details of the model Convivium from ARCLINEA.

2. CESAR produce this kitchen: Lucrecia. In the photograph at the bottom, a detail of the cooking zone.

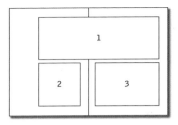

1. Lucrecia is a proposal from CE-SAR.
2. Detail of the cupboards with illumination from the model Lucrecia.
3. Some of the drawers of Lucrecia have two levels for the perfect organization of accessories.

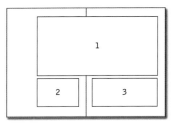

1. A kitchen from the brand POGGENPOHL.

2. Detail of one of the drawer utensil organizers with spice rack from POGGENPOHL.

3. Water and cooking zones from the model in photograph 1.

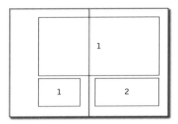

1. Largo is a proposal from LE-
   ICHT.
2. Pull out cupboards from the model Largo from LEICHT.

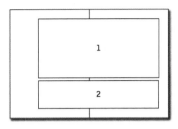

1. LEICHT include Ontario in their catalog.
2. Various details from the model Ontario. From left to right: the sink, a cupboard with the built-in oven and microwave oven and an interior view of some of the drawers with organizers.

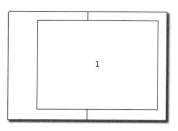

1. The model Largo in different colors, from the brand LEICHT.

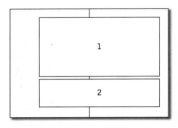

1. Ontario is a kitchen from LE-
   ICHT.

2. Detail of the interiors of some of
   the drawers from the model Ontario for cleaning products (left)
   and pots and pans (right).

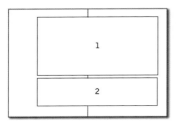

1. LEICHT present the kitchen Memori.

2. Various details from the model in photograph 1. From left to right: cupboard with raising glass doors, drawer organizers for accessories and utensils and sink.

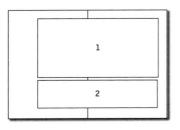

1. Model Ontario from LEICHT.
2. Different details of the model Ontario.

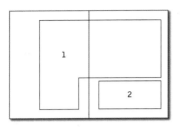

1. Different compositions proposed by BIS BIS KITCHENS.

2. Logica is a model from CUCINE COPAT.

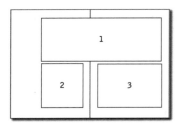

1. A proposal in a rustic style from LEICHT: Domus. In the photograph on the left, a detail of the glass cabinet.

2. Sink from the model Casa from LEICHT, also with a rustic air.

3. A combination of Largo produced by LEICHT.

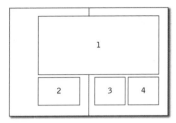

1. Model Como from the brand LE-ICHT.

2. Detail of the glass cabinets with interior illumination from Como.

3. In the kitchen Como, the cupboards and shelves are combined.

4. The kitchen Como is another proposal for rustic atmospheres from LEICHT.

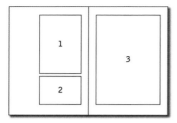

1. Larder from the brand POGGEN-POHL.

2. Cupboards with lattice doors, also from POGGENPOHL.

3. A rustic model from POGGEN-POHL.

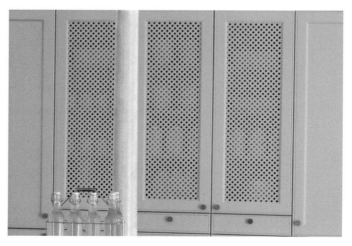

directory

ABC KITCHENS
Via Eritrea
20030 Seveso (Mi)
ITALY
Tel. 39 0 362 524 238
Fax. 39 0 362 551 745
info@abccucine.191.it
www.abccucine.it

AIKO CUCINE / ARCLINEA
ARREDAMENTI SPA
Viale Pasubio 50
36030 Caldogno (Vi)
ITALY
Tel. 39 0 444 394 333
Fax. 39 0 444 394 261
aiko@aiko.it
info@arclinea.net
www.aiko.it
www.arclinea.it

ALNO AG
Heiligenberger Str.47
88630 Pfullendorf
GERMANY
Tel. 49 07 552 21-0
Fax.49 07 552 213 4 00
mail@alno.de
www.alno.de

ALNO IBÉRICA
Príncipe de Vergara, 112
28002 Madrid
SPAIN
Tel. 34 917 451 223
Fax. 34 917 451 224
correo@alno.es
www.alno.es

ARCAYA EQUIP,
distributor in Spain for
DADA CUCINE
San Martín, 1 Bajo Trasera
01130 Álava

SPAIN
Tel. 34 945 462 408
Fax. 34 945 462 446
arcaya@jet.es

ARC LINEA ARREDAMEN-
TI SPA
(See AIKO CUCINE.)

ARRMET
Z.i. Via A.Volta, s/n
33044 Manzano (UD)
ITALY
Tel. 39 0 432 937 06-5
Fax. 39 0 432 740 102
mail@arrmet.it
www.arrmet.it

AURÓ CUINES
C/ Calderón de la Barca 1
08940 Cornellà de Llobregat
(Barcelona)
SPAIN
Tel. 34 934 743 696
Fax. 34 934 743 571
auro@auro-cuines.com
www.auro-cuines.com

BINOVA
Via Indipendenza, 38
60860 Assisi loc. Petrignano
Perugia
ITALY
Tel. 39 075 809 701
Fax. 39 0 758 097 020
www.binova.com

BIS BIS KITCHENS - BIS
BIS IMPORTS BOSTON
4 Park Plaza
2116 Boston
U.S.A.
Tel. 1 617 350 7565
Fax. 16 174 822 339

info@bisbis.com
www.bisbis.com

BLOCK COCINAS
Ctra. de Novelda a Aspe,
Km 5.8
03680 Aspe (Alicante)
SPAIN
Tel. 34 965 494 267
Fax. 34 965 494 426
correo@blockcocinas.com
www.blockcocinas.com

BLUM (Julius Blum GmbH)
Industriestraße 1
6973 Höchst
AUSTRIA
Tel. 43 5 578 705-0
Fax. 43 5 578 705-44
info@blum.com
www.blum.com

BONALDO
Via Straelle 3
35010 Villanova (PD)
ITALY
Tel. 39 0 499 299 011
Fax. 39 0 499 299 000
bonaldo@bonaldo.it
www. bonaldo.it

BOSSIA
Delegación Cataluña:
PLANAS GRUP
Riera de Fonollar, 13.
08830 Sant Boi de Llobregat
(Barcelona)
SPAIN
Tel. 34 936 529 306
Fax. 34 936 303 724
totbany@totbany.es
www.bossia.com

CASAWELL SERVICE
GRUPPE (WELLMANN)
Customer Centre
Industriestrasse 83
32120 Hiddenhausen
GERMANY
Tel. 49 05 223/1651 898
Fax. 49 05 223/165-51 460
info@casawell.de
www.wellmann.de

CESAR (Ver SMASHING
LINE.)
Via Cavalieri di Vittorio Vene-
to 1/3
30020 Pramaggiore
(Venecia)
ITALY
Tel. 39 04 212 021
Fax. 39 0 421 200 059
info@cesar.it
www.cesar.it

CONSENTINO SA
Ctra. Baza-Huercal Overa,
km. 59
04850 Cantoría (Almería)
SPAIN
Tel. 902 444 175
info@cosentino.es
www.cosentino.es
www.silestone.com

CONSENTINO USA, Inc.
13124 Trinity Dr.
Stafford, TX 77477
U.S.A.
Tel. 8 002 911 311
Fax. 2 814 947 299
www.silestoneusa.com

CONSENTINO UK
Unit 2, Octimum
Albert Drive

Sheer Water - Woking, GU21
5RW
UNITED KINGDOM
Tel. 44 (0) 8700 118 788
Fax. 44 (0) 1483 757 720
cosentinouk@silestone.com

CENTRAL EUROPE
Cosentino, NWE
Robert-Gerwig-Strasse 2
78244 Gottmadingen
GERMANY
Tel. 49 7731 976 790
Fax. 49 7731 789 312

CUCINE COPAT
Viale Lino Zanussi 9
33070 Maron di Brugnera
(Pn)
ITALY
Tel. 39 0 434 617 111
Fax. 39 0 434 617 512
info@copat.it
www.copat.it

DADA
Strada Provinciale 31
20010 Mesero
ITALY
Tel. 39 029 720 791
Fax. 39 0 297 289 561
dada@dadaweb.it
www.dadaweb.it

DONNA COCINAS
Polígono Industrial "La Fron-
tera"
Ugena (Toledo)
SPAIN
Tel. 34 925 533 200
donna@cocinasdonna.com
www.cocinasdonna.com

DRIADE
Via Padana Inferiore 12
29012 Fossadello di Caorso
(PC)
ITALY
Tel. 39 0 523 818 618
Fax. 39 0 523 822 360
www.driade.com

ELICA
Via Dante 288
60044 Fabriano (An)
ITALY
Tel. 39 07 326 101
Fax. 39 0 732 610 249
www.elica.it

ELMAR CUCINE (In Spain,
distributed by VERSAT)
Via E.Salgari, 18
31030 Biancade (TV)
ITALY
Tel. 39 0 422 849 142
Fax. 39 0 422 849 789
www.elmarcucine.com
www.versat.com

EUROMOBIL
Via Circonvallazione Sud, 21
31010 Falzè di Piave (TV)
ITALY
Tel. 39 04 389 861
Fax. 39 0 438 840 549
eurotec@euromobil.it
www.gruppoeuromobil.com

FRANKE S.A.U.
Polígono Can Magarola,
C/Molí de Can Bassa, 2-10,
Apto de Correos n° 174
08100 Mollet del Vallés
(Barcelona)
SPAIN
Tel. 34 935 653 535
Fax. 34 935 700 294
www.franke.es

FRANKE ITALIA
Via Pignolini, 2
37019 Peschiera del Garda
(VR)
ITALY
www.franke.it

GAMA-DECOR
Ctra. Viver - Pto. Burriana.
Km. 62
P.O. Box 179
12540 Villarreal (Castellón)
SPAIN
Tel. 34 964 506 850
Fax. 34 964 506 596
gama-decor@gama-
decor.com
www.gama-decor.com

LEICHT
Gmüder Strasse 70
73550 Waldstetten
GERMANY
Tel. 49 71 714 020
Fax. 49 7 171 402 300
Kontakt@leicht.de
www.leicht.de

LEICHT ESPAÑA
C/ Iglesia, 62
Apartado 108
08950 Esplugues de Llobregat (Barcelona)

SPAIN
Tel. 34 934 738 808
Fax. 34 934 700 242

MAGIS
Via Magnadola, 15
31045 Motta di Livenza
ITALY
Tel. 39 0 422 768 742-3
Fax. 39 0 422 766 395
info@magisdesign.com
www.magisdesign.com

MATTEOGRASSI
Via Padre Rovanati, 2
22066 Mariano Comense
ITALY
Tel. 39 031 757 711
Fax. 39 031 748 388
info@matteograssi.it
www.matteograssi.it

MOBALCO
Venecia 16
15940 Pobra do Caramiñal
(A Coruña)
SPAIN
mobalco@mobalco.com

NOBILIA
Waldstrasse 53-57
33415 Verl
GERMANY
Tel. 49 52 465 080
Fax. 49 5 246 508 117
nobilia@nobilia.de
www.nobilia.de

OSTER MÖBELWERKSTÄT-
TEN
Gewerbegebiet zur Höhe 1
56809 Dohr
GERMANY
Tel. 49 267 160 000

Fax. 49 2 671 600 090
moebelwerkstaetten@oster.de

PHILIPP PLEIN
Hebelstrasse 2
90491 Nürnberg
GERMANY
Tel. 49 01 805 468 374
Fax. 49 0 911 599 067
service@philipp-plein.com
www.philipp-plein.com

POGGENPOHL
Poggenppohlstrasse 1
32051 Herford
GERMANY
Tel. 49 5 221 381
Fax. 49 5 221 381 321
info@poggenpohl.de
www.poggenpohl.de

POLIFORM – VARENNA
Via Monte Santo 28
22044 Inverigo (COMO)
ITALY
Tel. 39 0 316 951
Fax. 39 031 699 444
info.poliform@poliform.it
www.poliform.it

POLIFORM Inc. – VAREN-
NA (ESTADOS UNIDOS)
150 East 58th Street
NY 10155 New York
U.S.A.
Tel. 212 421 1220
Fax. 212 421 1290
www.poliformusa.com

SIRA CUCINE
Via Fontevannazza, 9/A
62010 Treia (MC)
ITALY
Tel. 39 0 733 540 111
Fax. 39 0 733 215 030
info@siracucine.it
www.siracucine.it

SMASHING LINE
(Distribute CESAR
in SPAIN)
Montilla, 2, Polígono
Industrial Fontsanta
08970 Sant Joan Despí
(Barcelona)
SPAIN
Tel. 34 93 808 008
smashingline@teleline.es
www.smashingline.com

SMEG
Via Circonvallazione Nord,
36
42016 Guastalla (RE)
ITALY
Tel. 39 05 228 211
www.smeg.it

TECTA
Sohnreystr. 10
37697 Lauenförde
GERMANY
Tel. 49 0 527 337 890
Fax. 49 05 273 378 933
info@tecta.de
www.tecta.de

THE SINGULAR KITCHEN
(Central in SPAIN)
Plata 57
47012 Valladolid
SPAIN
Tel. 34 902 201 022

info@thesingularkitchen.com
www.thesingularkitchen.com

TONCELLI CUCINE
Via Gramsci, 19
56037 Peccioli (Pisa)
ITALY
Tel. 39 0 587 635 032
Fax. 39 0 587 636 410
info@toncelli.it
www.toncelli.it

VALCUCINE
Via Malignani 5
33170 Pordenone
ITALY
valcucine@valcucine.it
www.valcucine.it

VALCUCINE ESPAÑA
Berlinés, 9, bajos
08022 Barcelona
SPAIN
Tel. 34 934 184 695
Fax. 34 932 531 430
valcucine@ctv.es

VARENNA
(Ver POLIFORM.)

VINÇON
Passeig de Gràcia 96
08008 Barcelona
SPAIN
Tel. 34 932 156 050
Fax. 34 932 155 037
Barcelona: bcn@vincon.com
Madrid: mad@vincon.com
www.vincon.com